HIS TOT

Daily Reflections & Meditations on
The Body and the Blood of Christ

Ian Johnson
© 2015

HIS TOTAL PROVISION

Daily Reflections & Meditations on
The Body and the Blood of Christ

Ian Johnson.

**Published by
HAGM Publishing
4 Ewing Road,
RD4, Tuakau, 2694
New Zealand.**

E-mail ianjohn@xtra.co.nz

DEDICATION

This book is dedicated to the sisters of the Tyburn Monastery in Bombay New Zealand, who daily adore and reflect on the body and blood of Christ. The glory seen on their faces is what convinced me to pursue the total provision found in this meal.

HIS TOTAL PROVISION

1 Corinthians 10:16

The cup of blessing which we bless, is it not the communion of the blood of Christ? The Bread which we eat is it not the communion of the body of Christ?

Acts 2:46

And they continued daily with one accord in the temple, and breaking bread from house to house, they ate with gladness and singleness of heart.

Matthew 26:29

I say unto you, I will not drink of henceforth of this fruit of the vine until the day I drink it new with you in my Fathers Kingdom.

1 Corinthians 11:29-30

You should examine yourself before eating the bread and drinking the cup. For if you eat the bread or drink the cup **without honoring the body of Christ,** you are eating and drinking God's judgment upon yourself. That is why many of you are weak and sick and some have even died.

PREFACE

I love talking about the wonderful, supernatural meal that most in the Church call "Communion" Even as I wrote this little book my heart soared with excitement and thankfulness as I contemplate the meal that transports me back into the heart of the father.

I try to eat this meal in the natural on a daily basis, and my partaking in the spirit is a moment by moment reflection of his provision in my life.

After nearly forty years of walking in the faith, I have never tired of this meal, it is more desirable to me today than when I first began, because the more I eat it the more my DNA is changed and I appear in His image.

The scripture that comes to mind as I reflect on this meal and the provision found in it, is in the book of Psalms.

PSALM 20:4
May He grant you according to your hearts desire, and fulfill all your purpose in Him.

Some of you will be healed as you step into the total provision of His body and His blood. Some of you will find your true purpose in this life and the life to come.

My prayer is that you will all be blessed beyond measure as you learn to dwell in the total provision of Christ found in this meal.

As you eat and drink of this Eternal meal your DNA will be transformed and your earthly life enriched by its provision. Enjoy.

HIS TOTAL PROVISION

This book is a twenty one day devotional, why twenty One days? It takes twenty one days to form a habit. The aim of this little book is to form Christ in you through your habit of eating His flesh and drinking His blood on a daily basis.

The book is an invitation from heaven to partake of the greatest meal ever offered. My aim in writing this is to provide a daily reflection on the body and blood of Jesus. This reflection is just the beginning of your daily journey. Use the daily reflections to transport you outside of time and space and into the eternal realm. In that place seated with Christ, partake of the tree of life Himself. In time you will transform from one who has previously partaken of the tree of the Knowledge of Good and evil, into your true identity as a Son of Heaven, partaking of the tree of life.

In the book of John, Jesus issued the invitation to eat His flesh and drink His blood, The day he did that he lost many followers, then he turned to the twelve and said, "will you leave me also?" to which Peter replied "No Lord for you have the words of Life"

Jesus asks us the same question today; will you leave me also because of this invitation?" Remember the invitation to eat and drink of Him in the spiritual realm was given after Jesus had fed the five thousand in the natural realm. Those that followed Him could accept the natural provision, but not the invitation to eat and drink in the spirit, let us not be like these, but let us run into His invitation.

HIS TOTAL PROVISION

Before we start our journey together lets meditate and reflect on the key passage in John Chapter 6.

John 6:22-69 (NLT) The next day the crowd that had stayed on the far shore saw that the disciples had taken the only boat, and they realized Jesus had not gone with them. Several boats from Tiberias landed near the place where the Lord had blessed the bread and the people had eaten. So when the crowd saw that neither Jesus nor his disciples were there, they got into the boats and went across to Capernaum to look for him. They found him on the other side of the lake and asked, "Rabbi, when did you get here?" Jesus replied, "I tell you the truth, you want to be with me because I fed you, not because you understood the miraculous signs. But don't be so concerned about perishable things like food. Spend your energy seeking the eternal life that the Son of Man can give you. For God the Father has given me the seal of his approval." They replied, "We want to perform God's works, too. What should we do?" Jesus told them, "This is the only work God wants from you: Believe in the one he has sent." They answered, "Show us a miraculous sign if you want us to believe in you. What can you do? After all, our ancestors ate manna while they journeyed through the wilderness! The Scriptures say, 'Moses gave them bread from heaven to eat.' " Jesus said, "I tell you the truth, Moses didn't give you bread from heaven. My Father did. And now he offers you the true bread from heaven. The true bread of God is the one who comes down from heaven and gives life to the world." "Sir," they said, "give us that bread every day." Jesus replied, "I am the bread of life. Whoever comes to me will never be hungry again. Whoever believes in me will never be thirsty. But you haven't believed in me even though you have seen me. However, those the Father has given me will come to me, and I will never reject them. For I have come down from heaven to do the will of God who sent me, not to do my own will. And this is the will of God, that I should not lose even one of all those he has given me, but that I should raise them up at the last day. For it is my Father's will that all who see his Son and believe in him should have eternal life. I will raise them up at the last day." Then the people began to murmur in disagreement because he had said, "I am the bread that came down from heaven." They said, "Isn't this Jesus, the son of Joseph? We know his father and mother. How can he say, 'I came down from heaven'?" But Jesus replied, "Stop complaining about what I said. For no one can come to me unless the Father who sent me draws them to me, and at the last day I will raise them up. As it is written in the Scriptures, 'They will all be taught by God.' Everyone who listens to the Father and learns from him comes to me. (Not that anyone has ever seen the Father; only I, who was sent from God, have seen him.) "I tell you the truth, anyone who believes has eternal life. Yes, I am the bread of life! Your ancestors ate manna in the wilderness, but they all died. Anyone who eats the bread from heaven, however, will never die. I am the living bread that came down from heaven. Anyone who eats this bread will live forever; and this bread, which I will offer so the world may live, is my flesh." Then the people began arguing with each other about what he meant. "How can this man give us his flesh to eat?" they asked. So Jesus said again, "I tell you the truth, unless you eat the flesh of the Son of Man and drink his blood, you cannot have eternal life within you. But anyone who eats my flesh and drinks my blood has eternal life, and I will raise that person at the last day. For my flesh is true food, and my blood is true drink. Anyone who eats my flesh and drinks my blood remains in me, and I in him. I live because of the living Father who sent me; in the same way, anyone who feeds on me will live because of me. I am the true bread that came down from heaven. Anyone who eats this bread will not die as your ancestors did (even though they ate the manna) but will live forever." He said these things while he was teaching in the synagogue in Capernaum.

Many Disciples Desert Jesus

Many of his disciples said, "This is very hard to understand. How can anyone accept it?" Jesus was aware that his disciples were complaining, so he said to them, "Does this offend you? Then what will you think if you see the Son of Man ascend to heaven again? The Spirit alone gives eternal life. Human effort accomplishes nothing. And the very words I have spoken to you are spirit and life. But some of you do not believe me." (For Jesus knew from the beginning which ones didn't believe, and he knew who would betray him.) Then he said, "That is why I said that people can't come to me unless the Father gives them to me." At this point many of his disciples turned away and deserted him. Then Jesus turned to the Twelve and asked, "Are you also going to leave?" Simon Peter replied, "Lord, to whom would we go? You have the words that give eternal life. We believe, and we know you are the Holy One of God.

THE MYSTERY OF TOTAL PROVISION.

We are ever in HIM (Christ) yet always coming to HIM. We easily find HIM yet are always searching for HIM. There is no end of HIM. HE is God, and all of creation on earth & in heaven is in HIM. He is ever in us yet always calling to us. He hides from us yet stands in full view.

This is like a statement of the mysteries of God. We can know Him and yet we will never fully know him in this world because he is just too big to ever fathom. We find him in our searching and for a moment we are satisfied but then the ache to know him more begins its work in us and we start our seeking all over again. Scientists say that the universe is ever expanding and that makes total sense because God spoke all things into existence by His word and He has never said stop, so we can never really know the fullness of God because it's always expanding. He is in us and we are in Him so in a mysterious way all of creation is in us.

The bible says that all the hidden treasures of wisdom & knowledge are found in Jesus Christ and then it says all of Jesus is found in us and yet we struggle to remember where we left the keys. There is no paradox here because we are not God but the more we seek   Him and the more we abandon ourselves to Him, the more of us is found in Him and He in us.

Science struggles with the idea that we use only 10% of our brain capacity, but this only really tells us that the 90% is triggered by finding Him in us. Most scientific inventions and discoveries have been released by men & women who have a healthy belief in God. A Christian who is intellectually stagnant is not seeking nor abandoning them selves to the mind of the Lord.

Knowledge without revelation is stagnant water, we can even teach knowledge but the fruit it bears is simply knowledge. Revelation is imparted and expands our lives, opens up possibilities and transforms our world. The revelation of Christ within us is too big to view in its fullness, that's why we are called to meditate on Him and to enter into his thinking. We cannot enter into His thinking without laying down the pride of our own thinking, or enter into the fullness of a revelation without abandoning ourselves to the Lord of the revelation.

The answers to every mystery are found in Christ. That's why the bible says we can know in part and also says that when we see Him we shall be like Him for we shall see Him as He is.

The important issues of life are unlocked when we rest and abandon ourselves to gazing upon Him.

They are found in the communion in the body & the blood. In the communion there is total provision. Why? Because it is Jesus we are partaking of and in Him are found all the hidden treasures of wisdom and knowledge. In the communion there is total provision. He gave it all that we might gain all.

In partaking of the Body & the blood of Jesus we are entering into Him and affirming our covenant with Him and He is entering into us and all of the power of the Godhead is released in that meal. He drinks with us, thus fulfilling his words in Matthew 6:29. "I say unto you, I will not drink of henceforth of this fruit of the vine until the day I drink it new with you in my Fathers Kingdom."

It appears to me that the Church is neglecting the most important message; that all of the provision of God is found in Him and he offers this in the blood & the flesh of his own body freely.

That's why the bible says; **1 Corinthians 11:29-30** You should examine yourself before eating the bread and drinking the cup. For if you eat the bread or drink the cup **without honoring the body of Christ,** you are eating and drinking God's judgment upon yourself. That is why many of you are weak and sick and some have even died.

Some of you are sick and some have even died because you haven't discerned the body of Jesus. It's not a message of condemnation as some have made it. It's a message of invitation. It's a feast of the love of God, it's an invitation to enter into Him and He into us. It's in this mystical union that the fullness of Christ and all that means is found in the communion.

So I offer to you the invitation from God. "Come Eat my flesh & drink my blood, enter into the union of heaven and earth and be filled and satisfied."

The mystery is ever expanding every time you partake, being transformed and healed every time you eat and drink. Jesus called this the food and drink of heaven given by the father. It is perfect food because it comes from a perfect place.

12

It's not a monthly or weekly event; the early Church took it daily.

Acts 2:46 -And they continued daily with one accord in the temple, and breaking bread from house to house, they ate with gladness and singleness of heart.

We are called to live in this communion, it is a moment by moment event, and we continually live in the provision of the Body and the blood of Christ.

PERFECTION IS OUTSIDE OF TIME AND SPACE.
Perfection and sinlessness has to do with where we dwell and what tree we partake of.

Reflection on His body and His blood takes us outside of time and space and into the place where Jesus currently sits in eternity. The emblems we use on earth to bring us into remembrance are just that, emblems. The real transaction of communion takes place as we by faith partake of Him where He sits, at the right hand of the Father.

We must by faith enter that place (seated with Him) in order to step into the full provision found in the body and blood of Christ. We must understand that where he sits there is total perfection; in that place there is no sickness, suffering, sorrow or satan. So as we enter in the spirit, into that seat or throne where Jesus currently sits, what we partake of is more than natural food and drink, It is life. That's why Jesus said in John 6, If you eat this food you will never hunger again, and if you drink this blood you will never thirst again. Why? Because what we are partaking of is light from the tree of life, from the eternal realm.

In the beginning God created the heavens and the earth. The earth was without form, and void; and darkness *was* on the face of the deep. And the Spirit of God was hovering over the face of the waters. Then God said, "Let there be light"; and there was light. And God saw the light, that *it was* good; and God divided the light from the darkness. God called the light Day, and the darkness He called Night. So the evening and the morning were the first day. Gen 1:1-5 (NKJV)

To fully activate the creative voice of God found in the sound of his name we have to step out of time and into the dimensional realms of eternity hence the prayer Jesus gave to the disciples "As it is in Heaven so also on earth"

In Genesis one God spoke light out of himself – This eternal light is an expression of God – Time doesn't exist in this light, only God – In Genesis time didn't exist until day four of creation when he created the sun moon & stars to mark times & seasons. We don't need the Sun, Moon or stars for light they are just clocks and calendars and time pieces, that mark and contain both good and evil from the tree of the knowledge of good and evil in the garden. This tree has no access to any realm outside time.

The light in the voice of God transcends time and exists everywhere at all times and in all ways as his Illuminated self. When God speaks he brings His eternal light to the swirling mass of Kaos in our lives. It is in this light that the tree of life exists. God reintroduced the tree of life into time through Jesus. We don't have to wait for the right time or the right season, to partake of the tree of life, but we have to step into Him out of the dark swirling mass of time and the influence of the tree of the knowledge of Good and evil, - it is here where his voice illuminates. We

14

exit time and enter the light of His voice where the tree of life is.

This is the place of perfection, because it is outside time and space, there is no fall of man or rebellion of Satan in this place because all of that exists and is contained in time. We enter this light through the one who declared "I AM the Light of the World" His name is Jesus. In that place we are declared perfect because we dwell in HIM outside time and space and in this place we partake of the tree of life. John said sin has no place in us, and it doesn't when we are IN HIM. We are dwelling outside of time and space in him, and sin can only dwell in the dimension called time. So come out of the place called time and enter the light of His voice called eternity and eat His flesh and drink His blood.

It is an act of faith, what you see you can have, so by faith you need to see yourself in Him.

This book is for contemplation, meditation and reflection on the body and blood of Christ. Enjoy the journey.

The Church Fathers Said:

"I have no taste for the food that perishes nor for the pleasures of this life. I want the Bread of God which is the Flesh of Christ, who was the seed of David; and for drink I desire His Blood which is love that cannot be destroyed." **Ignatius of Antioch 80AD**

[Christ] has declared the cup, a part of creation, to be his own Blood, from which he causes our blood to flow; and the bread, a part of creation, he has established as his own Body, from which he gives increase to our bodies." **Irenaeus 177AD**

"The Word is everything to a child: both Father and Mother, both Instructor and Nurse. 'Eat My Flesh,' He says, 'and drink My Blood.' The Lord supplies us with these intimate nutrients. He delivers over His Flesh, and pours out His Blood; and nothing is lacking for the growth of His children. O incredible mystery!"
Clement of Alexandria 202AD

"'The cup of blessing which we bless, is it not communion of the Blood of Christ?' Very trustworthily and awesomely does he say it. For what he is saying is this: 'What is in the cup is that which flowed from His side, and we partake of it.' He called it a cup of blessing because when we hold it in our hands that is how we praise Him in song, wondering and astonished at His indescribable Gift, blessing Him because of His having poured out this very Gift so that we might not remain in error, and not only for His having poured It out, but also for His sharing It with all of us."- **John Chrysostom 392AD**

16

The Church Fathers Said:

"Thus, every soul which receives the bread which comes down from heaven is a house of bread, the bread of Christ, being nourished and having its heart strengthened by the support of the heavenly bread which dwells within it. **Ambrose of Milan 400AD**

"After the type had been fulfilled by the Passover celebration and He had eaten the flesh of the lamb with His Apostles, He takes bread which strengthens the heart of man, and goes on to the real Sacrament of the Passover, so that just as Melchizedek the priest of the Most High God, in prefiguring Him, made bread and wine an offering, He too makes Himself manifest in the reality of His own Body and Blood."
St Jerome 450AD.

"He who made you men, for your sakes was Himself made man; to ensure your adoption as many sons into an everlasting inheritance, the blood of the Only-Begotten has been shed for you. If in your own reckoning you have held yourselves cheap because of your earthly frailty, now assess yourselves by the price paid for you; meditate, as you should, upon what you eat, what you drink" **St Augustine 426AD**

DAY ONE

As I contemplate the body and the blood of Jesus, I am overwhelmed by the total provision found in Christ. Not only is it found in Christ but it is found in me as he shares of himself with all who will partake of this provision. The provision is so complete IN HIM that I get to put on the mind of Christ. I get to step into the fullness of all that fills all. I cannot say I am hungry when I am presented with such a meal, I cannot say "I thirst" when I have partaken of his nature and entered His thirst. I am full and I am satisfied IN HIM

2 Peter 1:4 NKJV by which have been given to us exceedingly great and precious promises, that through these you may be partakers of the divine nature.

Today my DNA is changed because I am a Partaker of the divine nature through this meal of His Blood and His body.

DAY TWO

As I contemplate the body and the blood of Jesus today. I take into myself HIS life, which is eternal. I am not dead in sin but alive in Christ. Jesus freely gave of himself to become my full provision of life. I am not subject to the law of sin & death but I live in His life which contains the law of liberty. Jesus Gave his life freely that I might have life.

John 10:18 - Jesus said: No one takes my life from me. I give my life of my own free will. I have the authority to give my life, and I have the authority to take my life back again.

No one killed Jesus, the Romans didn't, the Jews didn't, not even your sin killed Jesus - He freely gave his life in love and in the power of the resurrection he took it up again. Heavens passion is for me to step into this true resurrection life today.

\

DAY THREE

As I contemplate the body & blood of Christ,
I am reminded that I no longer live. I am alive but only
in him.

Galatians 2:20 I am crucified with Christ:
nevertheless I live; yet not I, but Christ lives in me:
and the life which I now live in the flesh I live by the
faith of the Son of God, who loved me, and gave
himself for me.

The life that I have is Christ's... I live by faith, but not
by my faith but by His faith. Even faith belongs to Him.
Jesus asks me not to work for, but to yield to his
embrace. To enter into life and it's fullness is to enter
into Christ and his fullness. To enter his faith is to
enter the faith that created everything. To enter his
love is to travel beyond human comprehension of
love. To enter his giving of himself is to enter divine
generosity.

DAY FOUR

As I contemplate the body and the blood of Christ, I
see that Jesus revealed that He is my total provision; I
can do nothing but feast on Him. –

John 6:35 then Jesus declared, "I am the bread of
life. Whoever comes to me will never go hungry, and
whoever believes in me will never be thirsty.

He says "if you eat my flesh and drink my blood you
will never hunger or thirst" and "if you eat my flesh
and drink my blood you will have eternal life" in fact
Jesus said it four times to reinforce the truth that
unless we Eat & Drink we won't have life.

It was a hard saying for many and they left following
Jesus that day. Jesus said to the Twelve "will you
leave me also?" To which Peter said "where will we
go- you are the Messiah –you have eternity in your
words"

Even when the words of Jesus the Messiah challenge
us to the core and we want to run, we remember it is
his body and his blood that sustains us and fills us
and brings us the provision of eternity Now. It's a DNA
exchange our corrupt DNA is exchanged for his
incorruptible DNA. Its an exchange of the records held
against us, for his perfect record. When we are found
in him the record of our DNA can be presented
without spot or wrinkle.
The hard saying is this, I can do nothing to gain
perfect incorruptible DNA by my own efforts. Only in
sharing the meal of his body and his blood can I walk
in his total provision. Religion rebels at this saying and
walks away.

DAY FIVE

As I contemplate the body & the blood of Jesus I am reminded of who He is. In my humanness I cannot comprehend this vastness; all I can do is abandon myself to Him.

Psalm 143:5- 6
I ponder all your great works. I think about what you have done. I reach out for you. I thirst for you as parched land thirsts for rain.

It's like falling headlong into a mighty flowing river. The thing about a river is that it will always find it's own boundaries nothing can prevent it's flow. We can dam it up for a season, but the flow will ultimately overwhelm it's gates.
To be carried away into intimacy with God Is to abandon ourselves to his purpose The rivers of God flow where He directs. We become possessed by that which we abandon ourselves to. Our heart desires to be possessed by Jesus when we view him through the love flow of his wounds, and enter into the provision of his body.

DAY SIX

As I contemplate the body and blood of Jesus I am reminded that the more I step into Him the more freedom I walk in. The hall mark of a yielded life is freedom. That's how we can measure the glory on our life as we move from glory to glory.

2Cor 2:17-18 Now the Lord is the Spirit, and where the Spirit of the Lord is, there is freedom. And we all, who with unveiled faces contemplate the Lord's glory, are being transformed into his image from glory to glory, which comes from the Lord, who is the Spirit.

The freedom comes because we cast off the constraints of the flesh and of our soul, as we enter into Him. We rediscover who we really are – The truth is His blood & His body take us through the veil and into His perfection. The veil is removed by the power of the blood and we see clearly the face and substance of The Lord. What we see is the same sight that Adam saw when breath first entered into him in the garden. As a result of this breath/sight Adam walked freely in the perfection of God. So the scripture above goes from being just words to being the DNA ladder through the body and blood of Christ into that freedom we all long for.

DAY SEVEN

As I contemplate the body and the blood of Jesus today I am reminded that Jesus multiplies the little that we have and brings an overflow into every aspect of my life.

John 6:9-13 - "There's a young boy here with five barley loaves and two fish. But what good is that with this huge crowd?" "Tell everyone to sit down," Jesus said. So they all sat down on the grassy slopes. (The men alone numbered 5,000.) Then Jesus took the loaves, gave thanks to God, and distributed them to the people. Afterward he did the same with the fish. And they all ate as much as they wanted. After everyone was full, Jesus told his disciples, "Now gather the leftovers, so that nothing is wasted." So they picked up the pieces and filled twelve baskets with scraps left by the people who had eaten from the five barley loaves.

Jesus lifted into heaven with thanksgiving that which he had (five loaves & two fish) and it multiplied enough to feed 5000 men & their woman & children with lots left over. Today as I reflect on the provision found in HIM, there is always going to be abundance as I partake of HIS body and HIS blood. My hunger & thirst is satisfied, I am full. The material, Spiritual, emotional and Physical needs I have will be satisfied in JESUS. The little that I have I lift into heaven with thanksgiving just as Jesus did until my baskets are overflowing. He invites me daily to Eat and to Drink, I come with thanksgiving and HE fills my baskets. His body and His blood are my abundance.

DAY EIGHT

As I contemplate the body and blood of Jesus I consider The manner in which he came into the earth and the power he displays to present me perfect.

Luke 1:34-35   Mary asked the angel, "But how can this happen? I am a virgin." The angel replied, "The Holy Spirit will come upon you, and the power of the Most High will overshadow you. So the baby to be born will be holy, and he will be called the Son of God.

This "overshadowing" is the same concept as is found in Genesis one "the Holy Spirit brooded over the face of the deep" out of the Genesis encounter came all of creation, where God revealed himself in his creation. Out of the Luke one encounter God revealed himself in His creature. He literally stepped into the womb of his creature. The DNA of Jesus is Holy (separate, set apart) it remained so during his earthly life and remains so even now. So as I partake of his body and his blood I too am "overshadowed" by the perfection of His DNA. The result of this overshadowing is a new creation formed in the perfect DNA of Messiah. Daily he is correcting my wrinkled and spotted DNA and I am formed without spot or wrinkle not by my strength but by the power of being overshadowed by Him.

DAY NINE

As I contemplate the body and blood of Jesus I am reminded that true intimacy is usually unseen by most of humanity.

In Israel I saw a little dear/goat like creature called an Ibex.. There were lots of baby Ibex with the heard. The thing about the Ibex is that they give birth in secret, no one knows where it happens, but the fruit of that secret place is obvious because of all the little baby Ibex.

Job39:1 "Do you know when the Ibex give birth? Have you watched as they are born in the wild?

The invitation to partake of His body and his blood is such an intimate and individual thing. The transactions that occur in these intimate moments although unseen become obvious because of their fruit. Like the Ibex those who share in an intimate relationship with The Lord through his body and blood have fruit that no one knows where it was birthed. The fruit of the Ibex is a little image of its parent, the fruit of our transactions of intimacy with The Lord is the image of Christ.

DAY TEN

As I contemplate the body & blood of Jesus, I am drawn to the wholeness of His body. That in His body is my total provision, in healing and indeed life.
1 Corinthians 11:24 NLT Jesus took bread and gave thanks to God for it. Then he broke it in pieces and said, "This is my body, which is given for you. Do this to remember me."

Note that the scripture says "This is my body which is given" some versions say "broken" which is a wrong translation of the Greek. We know from the scripture that not one bone was broken in his body... So we must be careful to discern the wholeness of the Lords body in order to receive wholeness. Many declare "This is his body which was broken" when they partake which is why Paul said "for this reason some of you are sick and some have even died because they have not discerned the Lords body" When we partake of His body we partake of the eternal unbroken provision of Christ. I take into myself the healing, deliverance and total provision found in his body, and I come into agreement with The Lord himself when He said "If you eat this flesh you will have eternal life".. NOW.

DAY ELEVEN

As I contemplate the body and the blood of Jesus, I consider the covenant formed in his blood.

1Cor11:25- "This cup is the new covenant in My blood; do this, as often as you drink it, in remembrance of Me."

When a covenant is cut it usually involves the promises of both parties. The exceptions are:

1) when God cut a covenant with Abraham he did so while Abraham was asleep, God passed between the two pieces of a sacrificed animal like a flashing fire and sealed the covenant without Abrahams promise. In other words it was a one sided unconditional promise to Abraham. Abraham was asleep and made no promises so nothing Abraham did could break the covenant.

2)The covenant cut by Jesus in his blood was also cut while we were asleep in our sins. Jesus sealed the covenant in an unconditional act of love. Abraham entered the promise while he was asleep in a dream. We enter into the promise of eternal friendship with God when we drink the cup in remembrance of all Christ did for us while we were asleep in our sins. The cup reminds me that his love demonstrated through the shedding of his blood is an unconditional love. He made all the promises while I was asleep in my sin. Today I enter into all the promises of God in Christ by his blood, not by anything I have done or will do, but entirely by the grace of God demonstrated in Christ for me.

DAY TWELVE

As I contemplate the body and blood of Jesus I am reminded that I abide in Him.

John 15:4- Abide in Me, and I in you. As the branch cannot bear fruit of itself unless it abides in the vine, so neither can you unless you abide in me.
The definition of "Abide" is - to continue to be present. Reflection on his body and his blood is not just a daily, weekly or monthly event. It is a continual awareness of our surroundings. In Him our motivation, our thoughts, our vision and sustenance are formed. To rest In Him is to be aware of where my fuel comes from. To gain vision in Him is to see from the place where he is seated. (at the fathers right hand) To walk in pure motivation is to step into the mind of Christ.

So today my reflection is not just in the moment of consuming the emblems. It is a deep transfer of life, love and glory. It is a daily encounter that fuels me; Spirit, soul and body. A vine bears fruit not through hard work, but by simply abiding in the source. So today I choose to continue to be present in Him.

DAY THIRTEEN

As I contemplate the body and blood of Jesus, I am reminded that He is the living bread given by the father in heaven. He is not words on a page; he is the full revelation of the voice of God. It is easy to fall into the habit of thinking that all my provision is in the Logos (Abiding written word) of God. When the Holy Spirit wants to lead us to the revealed word of God, Jesus)

Those around Jesus in **John chapter 6** said – All our ancestors ate bread in the wilderness, the scriptures say 'Moses gave them bread from heaven to eat' Jesus replied; Moses didn't give you bread from heaven – my father did; and now he offers you the true bread from heaven.

Isn't it interesting how they quote "The Scriptures" when in fact the scriptures didn't say that at all. It was easier for them to believe the Logos word (the written law) than to believe the Rhema word (Jesus) who was standing in front of them. We need to be reminded that the written word points us to the revealed word. In fact the word says "All the 'HIDDEN' treasures of wisdom and knowledge are found in Jesus"
Jesus goes on to say "He who eats this bread" (Partakes of HIM) will never be hungry again, then he says whoever believes in me will never be thirsty again.

DAY FORTEEN

As I contemplate the body and blood of Jesus, I am reminded that I am grafted into His vine.

John 15:5 "Yes, I am the vine; you are the branches. Those who remain in me, and I in them, will produce much fruit. For apart from me you can do nothing.

I am totally reliant on Him for my sustenance and my life. I bear fruit because I am eating and drinking of Him. Apart from the vine I am fruitless.

I choose to drink deep of the provision of His blood in the vine, and I choose to eat bountifully of His body in the Vine.

The key lesson is Abide and drink, If we just read and think we will fail and sink. The written word is not the forth member of the Godhead. It is the abiding word of God given to reveal the living word of God.
It's not Moses who is feeding us in the wilderness; it is the eternal revelation of Christ, the living bread that is feeding us.

DAY FIFTEEN

As I contemplate the body and the blood of Jesus. I am reminded of **Ephesians 1:4** He chose us in Him before the foundation of the world, that we would be holy and blameless.

Before there was original sin there was original perfection, He chose us IN HIM in this perfection. This grace is activated by faith. For by grace we are saved "through faith" many are putting their hope in the wrong place. We need to focus our faith IN HIM before the foundation of the world and become lost in his perfection and not wallowing in our sin in this realm. Before the creation of the world there was no sin suffering or sorrow; only perfection. This is the place we enter IN HIM by faith.. As we eat His flesh and drink his blood we are by faith transported into this place before the foundation of the world. That's why there is no condemnation IN CHRIST because in him there is nothing to judge us only our perfect Jesus.

DAY SIXTEEN

As I contemplate the body and blood of Jesus, I am reminded that in Christ I am a new creature.

2 Cor 5:17 Therefore, if anyone is in Christ, he is a new creation. The old has passed away; behold, the new has come.

In Quantum physics a frequency wave will continue in a direction uninterrupted until it encounters a frequency of a greater value. At a sub atomic level when a greater frequency is encountered the original frequency pops open and merges with the greater frequency and changes direction. The original change occurs when we turn our face toward YHVH, this is called repentance - When we partake of Christ by drinking his blood and eating his flesh daily we merge in Divine union with the greatest frequency of all. So powerful is this merger that we become a new creature, the old wave is broken and we resonate with a new sound. Instead of just sounding like an earth bound creature our sound IN HIM now contains the sound of a better covenant, a covenant sound that resonates out of Heaven. You can't hide in the spiritual realm you just need to resonate in this divine union. Creator and creature merged as it was in the beginning, you are not God but IN CHRIST. You carry His sound.

DAY SEVENTEEN

As I contemplate the body and the blood of Jesus. I am reminded of the words of Jesus.

John 10:9 9" Jesus said, I am The Gate; if anyone will enter by me, he shall live and shall go in and out and shall find the pasture."
Jesus also said in John 17 - I am in you and you are in me

It's a two way gate, we enter into him through the gate of his wounds, and He enters the world through us. That's why there is always a battle for the gates. It's a finished work on the cross and our access is by faith.. By grace I am saved - through faith. The enemy of our soul cannot deny us access, but he will try and obscure our view of the gate.

Jesus said that we come in and out - and find pasture.. When we enter into Him through the wounds of Christ we sit where he sits and see what He sees...When we come out we are as Christ to the world, because we have found pasture IN HIM. Eating his flesh and drinking his blood is our pasture. The battle of the gates is won by faith in his finished work on the cross. My entry into this pasture is not reliant on my goodness but on His, it's not reliant on my holiness but on his. The battle of the gates is a result of my response to His invitation to eat and drink.

DAY EIGHTEEN

As I contemplate the body and blood of Jesus, I see that his salvation is so complete that in baptism I died with him and in death I was buried with him.

I have been to the garden tomb in Jerusalem and it's empty. I could find no record of my former self who was buried there INHIM. The good news of salvation is that I was raised together with Him by the glory of the Father. The life I now live, I live IN HIM. I cannot be found in death.

Romans 6:3-4. - Are you unaware that all of us who were baptized into Christ Jesus were baptized into His death? Therefore we were buried with Him by baptism into death, in order that, just as Christ was raised from the dead by the glory of the Father, so we too may walk in a new way of life. Therefore we were buried with Him by baptism into death, in order that, just as Christ was raised from the dead by the glory of the Father, so we too may walk in a new way of life.

As I discern His body I see it is totally alive by the glory of the Father, so that which I eat and that which I drink is not subject to an old life, or to death. I no longer even breathe oxygen because my life is hid in Him and his breath reflects the father and he breaths glory and light. The record of my wrong doing is overwhelmed IN HIM. Our new way of life is outside of the law of sin and death because inside and out I am hid in Christ. I live in the law of liberty which has made me free.

DAY NINETEEN

As I contemplate the body and blood of Jesus, I see that I am fulfilling Hs word that we would partake of the fruit of the vine together in another realm.

Matthew 6:29. "I say unto you, I will not drink of henceforth of this fruit of the vine until the day I drink it new with you in my Fathers Kingdom."

The exciting thing about this journey is that we get to eat and drink with Jesus. It strengthens us and it blesses Him.

His desire is to share his glory with us, what better way to share an intimate moment. By eating and drinking together in Abba's Kingdom.

This scripture confirms for us that the place we eat and drink this meal is in Him.

DAY TWENTY

As I contemplate the body and blood of Jesus
I am rejoicing that daily I am learning that this meal is
my total provision. I am stepping into what the early
Church knew and experienced.

Acts 2:46 and they continued daily with one accord in
the temple, and breaking bread from house to house,
they ate with gladness and singleness of heart.

Singleness of heart is an interesting thought; we are
single in our thoughts because the truth is clear. IN
Christ this meal is our total provision. This is the most
important event of my day. I am being renewed and
transformed by this precious meal.

Gladness is welling up with in me now – I am healed, I
am satisfied, I am full, I am living in the total provision
of Christ.

I am continuing in unity with my creator and my
master to step into the total provision of Christ.

DAY TWENTY ONE

As I contemplate the body and blood of Jesus, I
reflect on the power and provision found in this meal.
I am made whole, healed and gain eternal life now
because of the power and provision found in his body
and his blood. I honour the body of Christ, it is all I
need it is my total sustenance, because of this I am
whole.

1 Corinthians 11:29-30 you should examine yourself
before eating the bread and drinking the cup. For if
you eat the bread or drink the cup **without honoring
the body of Christ,** you are eating and drinking
God's judgment upon yourself. That is why many of
you are weak and sick and some have even died.

The journey of this book is at an end, but your journey
is just beginning.

Thank you Lord that I am on my journey of discovery
now, and every day I come and explore the endless
provision found in this meal. Im getting stronger every
day because my DNA is renewed as I discern the
power and provision of this meal.

About the Author

IAN JOHNSON

Saved in 1977 as a result of a face to face encounter with Jesus, Ian Johnson has always sought to live in a life of encounter and intimacy with the Lord. With a heart for history, Ian has discovered that in every century the Church has demonstrated the supernatural. He has made it his mission to communicate the mystical and supernatural realm of the Kingdom of God to this current generation.

Ian has been in ministry for over twenty five years having pioneered and led Churches in the South Auckland area of New Zealand.

Ian and Joye Johnson travel as itinerant ministers speaking in Churches and conferences in NZ, Australia and the nations.

**OTHER TITLES BY
IAN JOHNSON**

HEAVENS SON'S REVEALED ON EARTH
Revealing the image of who we really are.

This book is designed to get you on the road to a supernatural lifestyle that will see the process of transformation from Christian to son of the Kingdom. All Sons and Daughters are called to walk with God and to enjoy the realms of heaven, but most importantly, we are all called to release heaven on earth. This just won't happen while we remain committed to a system that prevents the maturating of sons and daughters. The worlds are groaning for the revelation of the Sons of God and a system that acts as a gate keeper and not as a gate opener for the King won't enable us to see the need to walk where we are all called to walk. The Church is called to be that gate opener, and Fathers and Mothers in the Church are called to show the Sons and Daughters the gates. This book is an invitation to revolution and reformation in the body of Christ. Not to dismiss the Church, but to lift her up as the true gate opener, so that the King of glory may come in.

Available from Amazon or Amazon Kindle.
www.amazon.com

INTO THE HEART OF JESUS
A 21 day journey into an Intimate walk

This book is for personal use, or for use with groups in a retreat situation. It is based on the concept that if we come to Jesus, He will come to us. These very simple devotions are designed to open the door to intimacy with Jesus through experiencing His heart and entering the Glory Realm.

These principles of devotion are similar in structure to those used by St Ignatius Loyola in his 'Spiritual Exercises', first published in 1540. Those who used these for personal revival went on to spark significant moves of God in India, Malaysia, the Philippines, Indonesia and Japan. There was nothing in the spiritual exercises to suggest that the power of God would be released in signs, wonders and in raising the dead, but those who were influenced by them, ministered out of a pure love for Jesus, and saw some wonderful miracles as a result. Relationship sparked revival!

Nothing has changed, and personal revival still comes out of this relationship. The power is not in the book but in your heart response to the moving of the Holy Spirit. Therefore this book is nothing more than simple words. If you let the Holy Spirit water these words, revival will surely come to your heart.

Available from Amazon or Amazon Kindle.
www.amazon.com

OTHER TITLES BY
IAN JOHNSON

THE MIRACLES OF FRANCIS XAVIER
The Life and Miracles of Francis Xavier

This book is about the amazing life of Francis Xavier, missionary and pioneer to India, Sri Lanka, Malacca, Indonesia, the Islands of the Philippines and Japan. In the brief years between 1541 and his death in 1552 Francis saw thousands turn to Jesus; the miracles that followed his preaching of the gospel in these years are just like the book of Acts.

King John 3rd of Portugal was the sender who mostly financed Francis mission. Francis was the one who went and encouraged countless hundreds of others to do the same.

The aim of this book is to inspire your heart to missions, either as someone who goes, or as someone who sends. There are still millions who wait for the next Francis Xavier.

Available from Amazon or Amazon Kindle.

www.amazon.com

**OTHER TITLES BY
IAN JOHNSON**

GLORY TO GLORY
A Journey of Intimacy & Worship

In the beginning God created man to have fellowship with Him and to walk with Him in total intimacy. Adam and God, according to the book of Genesis, used to walk in the cool of the evening and have uninterrupted fellowship together. Jesus had made a way for us to walk in this kind of intimacy again. The book Glory to Glory is designed to inspire us into a deep hunger for this kind of intimacy. This is your invitation to journey into the very heart of the Father, and form a lifestyle of abandonment and worship. Enjoy the journey.

Available from Amazon or Amazon Kindle.

www.amazon.com

OTHER TITLES BY
IAN JOHNSON

GEMS FROM HEAVEN
A collection of quotes from Ian Johnson

I have written this little book to encourage you in your walk with Christ. In my time as a Christian I have had many encouragers along the way and they have built into my life and helped me find my way to the throne room of God. The last part of the book contains quotes and Gems from heaven that the Lord has opened my eyes to see.

My prayer for this book is that God will use it to inspire and encourage many souls on their own journey to the throne room.

IAN JOHNSON – 2012

Available from Amazon or Amazon Kindle.
www.amazon.com

**OTHER TITLES BY
IAN JOHNSON**

ANZAC's ISRAEL AND GOD
The ANZAC legacy & modern Israel

I wanted to write something that would help New Zealanders and Australians understand what the big deal is about the restored land of Israel. I Also what to convey the part, we as ANZACs had and will have in the process.

I've tried to share an overview of who modern Israel is and where they fit in God's end time economy.

Since 2009 we have been taking groups of NZ and Australian folk into the land of Israel, where they are able to see for them selves the historical places, but also to see how God is dressing the land in anticipation for the return of Messiah. We visit the 'living stones' in the Messianic and Arab Christian communities in the land and pray and declare that the role of the twin ANZAC nations is not yet ended in the process of restoration. Much of my desire to communicate the heart of God for Israel and the ANZAC nations has come out of these times in the land of Israel. I would like to personally invite you to come with us to the land of Israel on one of our tours, to soak up for your self the heart of God.

Available from Amazon or Amazon Kindle.
www.amazon.com

45

BOOKS BY IAN JOHNSON

All titles Available From
**His Amazing Glory Ministries
4 Ewing Road RD4 Tuakau
2694, New Zealand.**

**Published by
HAGM Publishers
Auckland
New Zealand.
www.hagmian.com**

**Ph (09)2368126
E-mail ianjohn@xtra.co.nz**

All titles also available at www.amazon.com as
Paperbacks or as an E-book.

His Amazing Glory Ministries

His Amazing Glory Ministries was founded by Ian & Joye Johnson who travel the nation of New Zealand & the nations opening up prophetic and supernatural understanding in the body of Christ. They are based in Auckland New Zealand. Ian and Joye speak at Church and conferences as a sought after prophetic and teaching ministry.

To book Ian Johnson for Church or Conference speaking or supernatural ministry training engagements Contact the ministry by E-mail ianjohn@xtra.co.nz

View our Web-site www.hisamazinggloryministries.org

His Amazing Glory Facebook page.

ISRAEL TOURS

Ian & Joye Johnson take regular tours to Israel and are experienced tour leaders. To be part of our next tour go to www.israeltours.co.nz

TURKEY BIBLE LAND TOURS
Come with us to explore the other Holy land, Turkey. Two thirds of the new testament was written either to or from what is modern day Turkey and the nation is rich in biblical history. To be part of our next tour go to our web site www.hisamazinggloryministries.org

FOR SPEAKING ENQUIRIES

IAN AND JOYE JOHNSON
His Amazing Glory Ministries

E-mail ianjohn@xtra.co.nz

4 Ewing Road, RD4,
Tuakau 2694
New Zealand

HIS TOTAL PROVISION

Daily Reflections & Meditations on
The Body and the Blood of Christ

42319990R00030

Made in the USA
Lexington, KY
16 June 2015